The Ebb and Flow
Of
Life and Family

ROLL WITH THE TIDE - RIDE THE WAVES

GO BEYOND ME
BOOK TWO

SUSAN STIVER

THE EBB AND FLOW OF LIFE AND FAMILY: Roll with the Tide - Ride the Waves.

Go Beyond Me Series, Book Two

Copyright © 2024 by Susan Stiver

Scripture taken from *THE MESSAGE*. Copyright © 1993, 1994, 1995, 1996, 2000, 2001, 2002. Used by permission of NavPress Publishing Group.

Scripture quotations taken from the (NASB®) New American Standard Bible®, Copyright © 1960, 1971, 1977, 1995, 2020 by The Lockman Foundation. Used by permission. All rights reserved. lockman.org

All photos taken by Susan Stiver or used by permission.

Cover Design by John Bryll Pulido; website: brilliantcover.com

Interior Design and Publishing by RLS Creativity Publishing https://web.actionera.com/RLSCreativity/

Paperback ISBN: 978-1-998542-07-9

E-Book ISBN: 978-1-998542-06-2

Dedication

This Book is dedicated to
Families - Yours, Mine, and Ours;
To parents -
Without whom none of us would be here;
And to our Heavenly Father
Who created us all!

Acknowledgments

I thank God for my family and friends
who have encouraged me to pursue my writing and art,
and to become all that I was created to be.
Special thanks to my husband, Don,
who saw me through God's eyes,
and was my biggest fan.

Contents

THE BREEDEN FAMILY

THE STIVER FAMILY

Introduction

Just like the movement of the ocean on the seashore,
families are in a constant state of change.
From the gentle rolling waves
to the tumultuous thunder of the tsunami,
so it can be in families.
Storms will cause the ocean to churn, the depths to surface,
the waves to crash onto the beach,
then the water recedes
leaving treasures on the sand.

Step into
The Ebb and Flow of Life and Family,
And find those treasures.

Within My Heart

Thank you, Lord, for giving me
The creative art of poetry.
Within my heart springs forth a song
To glorify You all day long.
Amidst the toil and strife each day
You gently guide me in Your way.
My praise to You will ever be
For by Your love, You set me free.

Teach Them

It is autumn now and I am old.
　　　Days are passed and time is gold.
I remember spending hours here,
　　　The spring and summer of each year.

Just watching as the water lay
　　　Much like a mirror of the day.
The birds would glide from tree to tree
　　　Singing all their songs to me.

Sing to these lads and please their ear.
　　　Teach them what you've taught me here.
Teach them life is far more than
　　　Things thought up by thoughtless man.

Days Gone By

The beaches are deserted.
_____What was once there, now is not._
The town is but a ghost town –
_____Quite an empty, lonely spot._
The buildings stand so lifeless
_____And the water lies so still._
Where did all the people go?
_____Where's the lights and all the thrills?_
This used to be quite the town –
_____Just the place for crowds and fun._
The hotels are locked and empty,
_____And the boardwalk scene's undone._
Days gone by now memories
_____Of how things used to be,_
Like shells upon the seashore
_____Carried off into the sea._

Ode to Ocean City, Maryland

One of our favorite places for a family vacation in the 1960s.

How Do You Say "Good-bye"?

How do you say good-bye to someone you love,
        Someone who's dear to your heart?
How do you let go of a hand
        That helped to give you a start?

How do you say just how you feel
        When tears begin to flow?
How do you turn and walk away
        When it's time to go?

How do you say, "You mean so much.
        Thank you for all you've done."?
How do you show what words can't say
        To that very special one?

How do you say "Good-bye to those days."?
        I can't! I shant! I won't!
How do you say good-bye to a friend?
        It's simple – you just don't!

Heart Language

Please accept my deep concern and love
Though silent it may be.
Know that with my heart I'm listening
As your heart talks to me.

I'll hear of deepest sorrows
And days that could have been.
I'll hear of how things used to be
And how they'll be again.

I'll hear the love two brothers shared;
The memories that they made.
Take comfort in these things so dear,
And know that memories never fade.

Yes, hearts have a language all their own
As they share what words can't say.
Please know that many other hearts
Are listening to yours today.

Precious People

God gives us precious people
Who touch our lives each day.
People who with just a smile
Speak more than words can say.

People whose sweet spirit
Is felt right from the start.
People who with kind soft words
Can heal a broken heart.

People who just by being
Make the world a better place.
People who with a gentle touch
Dry the tear from off a face.

Yes, God gives us precious people
With work for Him to do.
I thank the Lord for giving us
Precious people just like you.

Once Upon a Time

I looked into your eyes to see
    A glimpse of love that used to be.
I looked so deep my spirit fell –
    I only found an empty shell.

The heart was cold; the eyes were blind;
    A hint of life I could not find.
The person that I thought I knew
    Could not be found inside of you.

I sometimes wonder, as I do,
    If what I saw was really you.
Was the man I knew a fantasy
    On a steed to set me free?

Instead, I found my soul enslaved.
    You left me with my heart enraged.
The man I loved could not be you –
    The dream I had was never true.

<u>Set Free to Become</u>

Setting boundaries has set me free
  To become God's Tapestry.
Weave me, Lord, as You will
  Your praise and glory to fulfill.
Forgive my faults and many flaws.
  Purify me for Your cause.
Make me whole that all may see
  Only Christ who lives in me.

Surrender

Surrender's not a valiant word,
    Or a word that denotes strength.
It's not a word for power
    To armies of great length.
It's music to the enemy
    And those who lay in wait
For a prey as they grow tired,
    Doomed to meet their fate.
Surrender denotes failure
    When one doesn't understand
That there is strength in letting go
    To take hold of God's hand.

Weakness becomes power.
    All fear is turned to peace.
Sleepless nights transform to rest,
    Anxiety to relief.
There's healing in surrender –
    When surrender is to God.
He'll fight the battles for you,
    And over the enemies trod.
He'll lift you from the miry pit;
    Set your feet on solid ground.
He'll protect you with His armies
    Of angels all around.
Beneath His wing is comfort,
    And shelter from the storm.
Our gift to Him – surrender.
    His gift – safety from all harm.

Senseless

A battle rages inside of me
As to what is right and wrong.
I want to grey the black and white
Where lines are clearly drawn.

My wants become obsessions
That obscure my sense of sight.
Blurred vision helps me justify –
I can make the wrong things right.

"Right" for at least that moment
As I please my sense of touch.
The warmth of someone near me -
Am I asking way too much?

The taste of love is bitter sweet,
Like vanilla on the tongue.
Warnings fall on deafened ears –
The tale of woe unsung.

The scent of danger fills the air,
But my sense of smell is gone.
Once again I've left myself,
And willfully do what's wrong.

I stand and watch as every sense
Brings ecstasy to the flesh,
Only to face reality –
I'm putting my soul to death....

A painful demise to be sure –
What's worse I'm not alone.
The one with whom I'm dancing
Is truly not my own.

What right have I to do this thing
That once was done to me?
Turning hopes and dreams to ashes
And scattering memories.

There's no such right under the sun –
No reason to harm another.
What I have felt should not be shared,
Or borne by any other.

The hurt that fills my broken heart
Is only mine to bear.
Lord, help me stop this path of pain
And yield unto Your care.

Heal me of my bitterness.
Soften my heart of stone,
That I may serve You as Lord and King –
You and You alone.

Keep My Heart, God

Father God, please tell me why –
    Why must I be alone?
Haven't I learned my lesson?
    Do I have to be on my own?

Haven't I learned to keep You first?
    To seek Your Holy face?
Haven't I learned to rest in You –
    Held tight in Your arms of grace?

Isn't there a point along the way
    When I can have company?
Someone to share my joy and pain?
    Someone just for me?

Thought I'd found him once or twice,
    But my heart is breaking so.
A pain so deep – could it ever heal?
    I fear the answer's "No".

Father and Great Physician
    To You I bring my heart.
Please restore and mend it –
    Every torn and shattered part.

Henceforth I'll seek You daily
    With my heart in hand.
Knowing You're a patient God
    When I don't understand.

Focus

I see Your faithfulness
Time and again.
So why do I question
You, my dear Friend?
My eyesight fails
And my heart cries out –
My soul overwhelmed,
My mind filled with doubt.
Help me, dear God,
As I fall to my knees,
Unburden my heart,
Attend to my pleas.
Forgive me, Lord
For demands that I make.
Humble my heart
For Your Kingdom's sake.
Open my eyes
To see only You.
Purify my heart,
And my mind renew.
Let me see my life
In the light of Your grace.
Bowed low at Your feet,
I fall on my face.
Thank You, dear Lord,
That You're mindful of me.
Keep my focus true,
And my heart set on Thee.

A Mother's Prayer

To bring a balance
     Must there be a fall?
Can peace come without
     Chaos after all?

How can we know
     God's love and truth,
Unless through trials
     He gives us proof?

Most gracious God,
     And loving Father,
Help this Your child
     To be a mother.

Mother's Day Letter to My Children

Because of you both, I'm a mother.
God blessed me with each of you.
I may not have all the answers,
Or always know what to do.

I thank the good Lord in His wisdom,
That in His great work is a plan.
Our future is sure because of His love –
He holds us close in His hand.

In His grace He guides if I follow.
When I fall, He patiently waits.
In His mercy He leads me through valleys,
To pastures outside of the gates.

I pray that the Lord will protect you
As you face the world on your own.
I pray that the Lord will direct you –
With Him you're never alone.

Learn early to lean on the Father's arms;
To rest beneath His wings.
Take comfort in His loving care,
For He provides all things.

Learn, for you may one day be
A father, and mother too.
May God bless you throughout your lives
As He's blessed me with you.

12 May 1996

Lessons from the Cherry Tree

Remember when we were so little
  And everything else seemed so big?
When life was a bowl full of cherries
  And into the bowl we would dig?

We were too young to notice the pits,
  Or to know that one day they'd be
The seeds from which our young children
  Would grow their own cherry trees.

I thank the Lord for the trees and fruit –
  For even the very pits.
I thank Him that in His loving care
  He makes all the loose branches fit.

Were it not for the pit, there'd be no tree
  Which by our Lord would root.
Were it not for the Loving Gardener
  Our tree would bear no fruit.

I thank the Lord for lessons I've learned
  From a simple cherry tree.
That He has a plan for our future
  Far greater than all we can see.

Daughter

Daughters are a special treasure
Sent from God above,
Filling life with joy and pleasure
Tenderness and love.

Daughter, you've brought all of these
Since the day you came –
A ray of light into my world,
Not a flicker, but a flame.

Each new day is an adventure.
It has been from the start.
With tears of joy when you were born,
You stole my very heart.

Yes, daughters are a precious jewel –
As in an oyster there's a pearl.
My life is rich because of you
My precious little girl.

Time has passed and you have grown
More beautiful and dear.
And with you grows your tenderness
And love with passing years.

Keep your heart in tune with God
And seek His will to do.
He'll show you how to use the gifts
That He has given you.

2 August 1996

Life's Blueprint

How can this be –
    Two hearts beat as one?
Battles are fought –
    The victory's won?
Minds set on You
    Are melded together?
Friendships are made
    That will last forever?
How can this be –
    So perfect a plan?
The blueprint of life -
    Drawn by Your Hand!

Thank You, Father God,
Author and Finisher of our faith.

Do Over

If I could do life all over again,
    I'm not quite sure where I'd begin.
Would I go back to one, two, or three?
    At just what point did I become me?

Playing in tents, and learning to skate,
    I remember the wonder of being eight –
Sledding in winter, roses in spring...
    Life was so full of every good thing.

Then came the teen years, and life took a turn.
    There was so much more for me to learn.
How could I grasp this thing called "life"?
    I finished school and became a wife.

My career defined one part of me –
    That inner part that most can't see.
Facing life with joy, and death with tears –
    That's who I was for all those years.

Into the mix some blessings came;
    My life would be forever changed...
A son and a daughter born to me –
    A mother I will always be.

Then a partner change, by God's design,
    I am his and he is mine.
Now fireside winters, flowers in spring...
    Life is so full with every good thing!

Hand in Hand

Father, thank You for this precious gift –
    Someone to have and to hold.
Help me keep my focus on You
    And my witness to be bold.

Thank You for this godly man
    Whose heart is stayed on You.
Help me lift him up in prayer
    Each day, the whole day through.

Help me not take for granted
    Any moment of his love.
May I never forget this treasure
    Is sent from You above.

Grant us wisdom as we seek Your face,
    Grace to understand,
Strength to face what lies ahead,
    As we go hand in hand.

Father, fill us with Your love
    So that our lives will be
Wholly acceptable unto You,
    And a loving reflection of Thee.

Wedding Vow

To Don

As your friend and companion
> *I come to your side*
Before God to pledge,
> *all my love, as your bride.*

I will cherish and love you
> *Till death do us part*
With God as my strength
> *From the depths of my heart.*

This treasure we're given -
> *"to have and to hold",*
Is a gift far more precious
> *Than silver or gold.*

To God be the glory
> *Great things He has done –*
From two separate lives
> *Our God will make one.*

Then from four separate lives -
> *We're created to be*
An expression of God's love
> *As one family.*

Family Prayer

Father, may our prayer as a family be –
    That our lives would reflect and glorify Thee.
Make our eyes quick to see the needs of another;
    Our ears swift to hear the cry of a brother.

Make our mouths sure to speak of Your mercy and grace,
    Displayed by the peace and the smile on our face.
Make our arms strong to hold the weak and the weary;
    Our hands gentle to wipe the cheek of the teary.

Make our legs as Thine own to carry about
    The message of joy, and of hope without doubt.
Make our hearts ever pure so the whole world will see
    Your goodness and love – the essence of Thee.

Check In Time

Check-in time is 4pm
    In most places where people stay.
Hotels, motels and the like,
    Make the rules that way.

But this is not The Hilton,
    Or The Holiday Inn,
So together let's come up with
    An appropriate time to check-in.

Morning is good – "Have a great day!"
    With happiness be on your way.
Afternoon works – "How's your day shaping up?"
    What a great pick-me-up!

Evening news and stories to share –
    Are another way to say "I care."
Night time wishes for dreams come true –
    A quiet prayer of gratitude.

So let's not miss the chance to say
    "I care about you" all through the day.
The best time to check-in? – without a doubt –
    Is all day long, and before checking out!

Inside Out

Wake me up, O God!
> *Stir my heart to beat like Yours.*
Let me hear Your voice
> *Like the waves upon the shore.*

Show me what You see
> *When You look throughout the earth.*
Make my eyes behold
> *The new thing You wish to birth.*

Awaken the compassion,
> *Set my heart aflame.*
Turn me inside out
> *To the glory of Your Name.*

In The Corner

When you're backed into a corner
  Remember that Christ is the Cornerstone.

Keep Him at the center of your life
  And His love at the center of your marriage.

Then come out of the corner
  One with the Father, and at peace with the world.

In Silence

Sometimes we have to feel what we cannot hear...

❤️ *Feel God's arms*
　　　around you as He caresses you with a hug
❤️ *Feel God's breath*
　　　on your cheek – the very breath that gives you life
❤️ *Feel God's strength*
　　　as He protects you under His wing
❤️ *Feel God's warmth*
　　　as He draws you closer to His side
❤️ *Feel God's love*
　　　as with every beat of His heart He declares His
　　　love for you.

Trust in these truths.
Rest in this wonderful relationship.
Know Him as Loving Father and Restorer of your soul.

In silence God speaks volumes
　　　He calls us to draw near.
But it's far more than His voice
　　　That He wants us to hear.

It's tenderness and laughter,
　　　Compassion from above,
The heartbeat of Almighty God
　　　Spells out His endless love.

Waiting

Waiting
- The most difficult thing to endure
- The easiest thing with which to be stuck
- The strongest thing against which to fight
- The hardest thing in life to do!

Time

Time you are unkind to me
- Too fast when I wish you to linger.
- Too slow when I wish you would flee.
- Too loose when I wish to be scheduled.
- Too confining when I wish to be free!

God Reaches Out

A mother's heart is breaking –
      The "perfect plan" has changed.
All that was supposed to be
      Is suddenly re-arranged.

With all hope and expectation
      A beautiful child was born.
But the course was changed on this voyage
      And the sails are nearly torn.

Tossed to and fro by frustration
      The sea of fear and anger swells.
Then the storm takes hold of the weary ship
      And batters the hearts as well.

In fear we cry out, "We perish!
      Someone, please, rescue me!"
In that instant is felt the grip of a hand
      In the midst of the stormy sea.

Did the storm stop? No, it rages!
      And it's not part of the "perfect plan",
But God reaches out through a mother's heart
      And touches you with her hand.

Take comfort in that mother's touch.
      Remember she's hurting too.
Then seek the very heart of God
      And trust Him to carry you through.

Wherever You Are

Papa God,

Wherever You are
    You take me there.
You leave me not
    In my despair.
You keep me in
    Your loving care.
For where You are
    You take me there.

The World Can Wait

This is my time
      The world can wait –
I'll wrap you in my arms.

I'll hold you close
      And sing you songs.
I'll guard you from all harm.

For all too soon
      You'll grow up,
And leave this warm embrace.

Hold close the love
      You've felt right here,
And know the world can wait.

<u>Gone Are the Days</u>

Gone are the days of little boy laughter...
> *Laughter so contagious - it infects the masses.*
> *Laughter so simplistic - and yet so profound.*
> *Laughter so innocent - it cannot be defiled.*
> *Laughter so sincere - it captures the heart.*
> *Laughter so other - it cannot be defined – it can*
> > *only be caught – Caught from the little boy in*
> > *whom laughter never dies!*

Embrace the days of little boy laughter!

To Todd,

whose little boy laughter will always be a gift that only he can share,

the treasure that only he can impart to the generations to come.

The Artist, Our Father

Did you see the sky today?
     Purple, blue and white.
The art of God just to say,
     "Everything's alright."

God paints His love in the sky
     For everyone to see,
And through the storms that come and go,
     He comforts you and me.

So, rejoice in the sun, the clouds and storm.
     Sing in the rain that falls.
Remember the Artist who paints the skies
     Is Heavenly Father over all.

If I Knew

If I knew when last I hugged you
  It'd be the last time in my life,
I would have hugged you all the tighter
  And even long into the night.

I'd have held you till my strength was gone
  And my heart would fail to beat.
That's how a mother loves her child –
  Near or far with memories sweet.

Life's Choice

Once again, the enemy has reared its ugly head in an
attempt to divide this house. It has rumbled from
beneath in an effort to crack the foundation.
It has surfaced from within seeking to shake the security,
break the spirit, and destroy the soul.

It has no regard for truth, freedom, peace or love.
It thrives on deceit, bondage, chaos, and broken rela-
tionships.
It is powerful and subtly destructive, but it can only
succeed if we choose to let it.

I choose to stand firm in Jesus Christ –
My Rock and my Salvation!
I claim the Victory in Him
As I stand on His promises!
I continue to press on to know the Lord
Lifting my voice to Him in praise!

"So let us know, let us press on to know the Lord.

His going forth is as certain as the dawn;

And He will come to us like the rain,

Like the spring rain watering the earth."

Hosea 6:3 (NASB)

Friends for Eternity

In the blankness on the page
    Please read what's in my heart.
So much love and gratitude –
    There was no place to start.

Between the lines are joys and tears,
    Happiness and pain.
Were it mine to choose the fate,
    I'd do it all again!

For on that page God wrote a note –
    To which He knows the end.
Into my heart He wrote your name,
    And beside it He wrote "Friend".

Love Knots

"Love Knots" the way God meant them to be
      Are entwined with no ill between you and me.
It's being bound together for a common cause –
      No rules, regulations or hard-to-keep laws.
It's consideration one for another.
      It's abandoning "wants" for love of the other.
It's freedom to be myself without fear.
      In spite of my faults, God still calls me "dear".
It's learning to walk hand in hand, side by side –
      Caring more for my friend than my foolish pride.
It's stopping to notice the hurt and the pain –
      Addressing the problem, and starting again.
It's singing and dancing when the storm's finally passed.
      It's holding on tighter when the storm has to last.
It's contentment in knowing the joy and the peace
      That comes from surrender – a bless-ed release.

Yes, "Love Knots" are blessings, rare treasures to find –
      Gifts from our God who is faithful and kind.
So, take hold of the knot and trust it to stay
      As tight as God made it, and as sure as the day.
A cord of three strands is not easily broken –
      Live in this promise that our Father has spoken.

My Dreams for You - *A mother's declaration of love.*

What was I thinking all those years ago
      When I first gazed upon your face?
Could I know where we'd be at this point in time?
      Could I ever have imagined this place?

A time when we can't see eye to eye,
      And heart to heart can't speak.
A time when truth is twisted,
      And when the lies at best are weak.

Was this what I hoped and prayed for –
      That our lives would be so estranged?
Was the joy in my heart short of target?
      Have my dreams for you ever changed?

Always praying that you'd know the Father
      I watched as God did His part.
Always watching with anticipation,
      I prayed that you'd give Him your heart.

What was I thinking all those years ago
      When I first gazed upon your face?
That you would live free in the truth of God's light,
      Daily growing in wisdom and grace.

Have my dreams changed for you from that day till now?
      Will they stand even under this test?
The heart of this mother will pray for her son –
      Asking for nothing short of God's best!

Between the Storms

Couldn't we dwell between the storms
And stay out of harm's way?
Couldn't we just play in the sand
And ride the waves all day?

Couldn't we laugh a little more –
Without a fret or care?
Couldn't we find that place again?
I want to go back there.

Yet without the storms there'd be no rain;
Without the rain – no sea.
Without the sea – no need for a beach
And then where would we be?

It seems I speak in circles,
And in other shapes and forms –
So wet or dry, I choose to dance with God
On the beach amidst life's storms.

A declaration of choice

Wrong Question

What's it all for?
> *Father, it hurts!*
You know I've tried,
> *But nothing works!*
The words are harsh.
> *The silence screams loud!*
Can't anyone see?
> *I'm alone in the crowd.*
Why go any further?
> *What's it all for?*
Seems I've passed
> *This way before.*
Where can I go
> *To find my rest?*
Then You lay my head
> *Upon Your chest.*

Hearing Your heart
> *I re-a-lize*
My question is wrong,
> *And to my surprise....*
You whisper softly
> *In my ear*
"When you ask the right thing,
> *All becomes clear."*
Who's *it all for?*
> *Father, now I see –*
It's all for You,
> *Because You love me.*

Carry Me Home

Carry me home on silver wings
    That lift me in the air.
My heart is full and joyfully sings.
    Protect me in Your care.

Take me home to the one who loves You
    With a love that overflows.
How blessed I am – he loves me too!
    And all of Heaven knows!

O Father, Giver of all good gifts
    How can I thank You enough?
My voice I'll raise and my hands I'll lift
    When the seas are calm or rough.

Beach to mountains – take me home.
    Complete this journey's end.
Carry me home to the arms of my love –
    My husband and my friend.

Precious Gifts

Precious Gifts

Is it Christmas at Thanksgiving?
How can this be so?
You've brought me very precious gifts
More precious than you know.

The Father heard this mother's heart
And decided what to do –
He sent me gifts abundant,
And delivered them through you.

Ones of every size and shape;
Ones with joyful sounds;
Ones to bless for years to come;
Ones to put my arms around.

These are treasures of a special sort –
None too loose or snug;
Just what a mother always needs –
The gift of children's hugs.

warm hugs

Hugs Are HUGe!

Hugs Are <u>HUG</u>e!
They're healing to the wounded,
        Comfort to those grieve,
Hope to the lost and hopeless,
        An embrace that's hard to leave.

HUGS are a gift that is .....
        Joy generating
        Energizing
        Stress relieving
        Anger disarming
        Faith building
        Tangible evidence of God's love
(I am intentionally leaving you space here, so that you can
        add to this list)

- Hugs speak LOUD without saying a word!

- My husband, Don, taught our children and grandchildren to give what he called "strong muscle hugs" – the tighter the better. Oh, what joy it generated!

- Consider this, the closer the better – leaving no room for ill between you and me. Heart-to-Heart communication. What a beautiful and powerful expression of love!

- Be sure to give and receive hugs as often as you can - especially in these days!

NEVER UNDERESTIMATE
THE POWER OF A HUG!

Forever♡

From the Mouths of Babes

It's fun to hear what children say -
Their little unfiltered words,
Expressing what they thought they heard
Amidst our grown-up world.

Capture and remember
The words, and stories, too!
Then, jot down all the special ones
That captured and tickled you.

Here's some special words used by our children and grandchildren.

Shelly's word for air conditioner was "ishcadisher"; and one of her powerhouse statements was "You're not the boss of me!"

Holly would often lead out her conversations with, "Dad, hope you know...."

Joe was a fixer – he just needed the right tool. When the adults couldn't seem to fix it, Joe would ask for a "toobiter" (translated screwdriver). He was confident he could fix it.

Ephraim was a warrior. He didn't use many words, but he could swash-buckle better than the rest. He also helped his older brother comes to grips with passing Socko, a multicolored teddy bear, down to a cousin with the simple statement, "It's got pink on it". Socko became history.

Sean, determined that he was correct by asking for a "Coca Colick", and frustrated with being corrected several times with the words "Coca Cola" finally braced his hands on his hips and blurted out, "NO, SPRITE!"

One daughter's word was "comterful". She could snuggle up and get comfortable, but just couldn't get all the letters arranged quite right to say it. And the old saying: "Six of one, half dozen of the other" came out anything but that.

Zane, at 3 years old, asserted his independence by stopping abruptly, raising his hand to stop his father from following him, and adamantly announcing "I do it myself!" That memory was topped only by his dressed-up appearance as a pirate during Christmas cookie baking when he raised his Styrofoam sword, and gruffly declared, "Sugar me timbers!" Of course, we obliged him with cookie booty.

Malachi didn't miss a trick, and was quick to catch his "tricky Grand-dad". The first sentence we heard him structure had to do with metal yard birds that were missing from the garden. Weather worn, they had been moved into the shop for repair. Seeing their perch, but not the birds, Malachi asked, "Where go birds?" He's still a stickler for detail.

Ruth Anna, at 3 years old, blessed us with advice and assurance to last a lifetime. Fixing her mother's hair, she told her to "Relax", "Don't be dared (scared)" "Nip, nip, nip... You're all ixed (fixed) up."

We have such wonderful memories and so much to be grateful for – straight from the mouths of babes!

**Prodigal's Parent, Know that God Cares**

Prodigal's parent –
>_Watch and wait._
Fall on your knees,
>_Look to the gate._

Prodigal's parent –
>_Cry out and plea._
Pour out your heart,
>_Trust God to heed._

Prodigal's parent –
>_Now quiet your heart._
Know that our God
>_Is doing His part._

Prodigal's parent –
>_Allow God to fill_
You with joy and hope –
>_Look to the hill._

Prodigal's parent –
>_Prepare to receive_
The blessings of God
>_Because you believe._

Prodigal's parent –
>_Watch as she comes._
Open your arms,
>_Welcome her home._
Prodigal's parent –
>_Praise God above_
As He pours out
>_His mercy and love!_

The Line's Being Drawn

The line's being drawn
Between darkness and Light.
The line's being drawn
Between wrong and what's right.

The line's being drawn –
Willful blindness or sight?
The line's being drawn –
Will you cower or fight?

The line's being drawn.
It's a line in the sand.
The line's being drawn.
On which side will you stand?

<u>Heal the Wounds</u>

Father, You are in this place –
*   Your presence is so real.*
I feel Your hand upon my head
*   As You begin to heal*
This wounded child within me
*   Whose heart cries day and night.*
Show me when to follow,
*   And teach me when to fight!*

Draw me close to hear Your heart
*   As I gaze into Your face.*
Rock me in Your arms of love
*   And the warmth of Your embrace.*
Then by Your hand transform me –
*   heal the wounds, erase the scars.*
Make me a living testament
*   Of the Loving God You are!*

Sean Matthew

Thirty years ago today
    A baby son was born.
My whole life was ever changed,
    And I was not forewarned.

How could I know my heart would grow
    To take this new child in?
How could I know the pride and joy
    That I would find in him?

How could I know the sleepless nights
    Would ever end in rest?
How could I know that all I'd do
    Would be the very best?

How could I know I taught him right
    And he'd know right from wrong?
How could I know it wasn't me,
    But You his whole life long?

You, O GOD, created him
    And grew this mother's heart.
You filled me with a mother's dream
    And helped me do my part.

Pour into him all the love
    A husband and father needs.
Then hear his heart as he cries out,
    And for his family pleads.

Answer his prayers so he will know
    With absolute resolve
That You're at his side in battle
    And the mystery's not his to solve.

Now take this man You gave to me
    I give him back to You.
Fill him with all strength and courage
    And a heart of worship too.

Love, Mom
December 25th, 2011

Zane's Poem

Made to ride – it's in my bones.
My Dad and Mom ride, too.
Made to ride – it's in my heart.
My grandparents are riders, too.

Made to ride – so in God's wind,
His Word my map and guide,
I mount my chrome and metal steed,
For I was made to ride.

2012

The Blessing of Family

Together we have laughed and cried, loved and lost, yet through it all we have endured and uplifted each other.
I will forever be grateful to God for this union, and the blessing of family!

THE BREEDEN FAMILY

Dad

Dad, sometimes I sit confused,
      And wonder if you wonder,
Just who I am and where we are? –
      Sometimes I sit and ponder.

I think you know my inner thoughts –
      What makes me be "me".
I think you know what's in my heart –
      When even I can't see.

A better listener I'll never find.
      You listen deep and long.
You hear much more than other Dads –
      Correct me, if I'm wrong.

Your quiet ways and gentleness
      I never understood.
You took the blame for all my mess.
      I'd fix that if I could.

∗

But in your ways you taught me
*   The things I'd need to know.*
And when I chose to leave the nest,
*   You smiled and let me go.*

You let me go, but never left me,
*   And every now and then,*
A timely call, your quiet voice
*   Gave me time to count to ten.*

You remind me that I'm part of you,
*   And you a part of me.*
I thank the Lord that in His wisdom
*   He gave you Sue Marie.*

That was my Dad, and I am so very grateful!

All About Family

Family was always important
_   To Mom and Dad._
We didn't have much –
_   But we shared what we had._

We learned to respect
_   Our Father and Mother,_
And we learned to love
_   Our sisters and brother._

We were taught that the truth
_   Was best to be told;_
That riches were far more
_   Than mere silver and gold._

We were given wise counsel
_   To teach us good sense._
We were given life's boundaries –
_   But never a fence._

Our home, a safe haven –
_   God gave us the best!_
Love was the constant
_   Through which we were blessed!_

So grateful for our parents and our family.

Christmas Was Special

Christmas was special
     The tree and the lights,
The train set was perfect,
     The tunnel – just right.

But what made it special?
     Not lights, nor the tree,
Not the cookies or presents –
     Not the things you could see.

What made it special
     Was the warmth in the cold,
It was time spent together –
     More precious than gold!

Christmas was special
     And will always be,
Because Mom and Dad gave us
     Such sweet memories!

Different but the Same

Sisters, we three
*   With one Mother, one Dad*
Such different lives
*   Each of us had.*

High expectations,
*   Grace without measure.*
The good and the bad times,
*   Memories to treasure.*

Unique in ourselves
*   Yet each of us one.*
We learned how to laugh
*   And how to have fun.*

We learned how to share
*   And love one another.*
But we weren't alone –
*   We, too, had a brother.*

Siblings, we four
*   With one Mother, one Dad*
Such different lives
*   Each of us had.*

Our Mother's Hands

Remarkable hands –
    The mark of a mother.
They cooked and they cleaned –
    And prayed like no other.

Hands that made meals,
    Painted walls, sewed our clothes,
Hands that made cookies,
    Wrapped packages with bows.

Hands never idle –
    Now still in her lap.
A Mom always busy –
    Now down for a nap.

Help me remember
    The holidays past,
The good – not the bad,
    The first – not the last.

For mom, give her peace,
    And grant her sweet rest.
Fill up her world
    With all of the best.

Take her to times
    When we laughed and we played.
Erase all the turmoil
    And the hardest of days...

Then grant us the grace
To join her there –
Wherever she is,
Keep her safe in Your care.

Yes, remarkable hands –
But that's only one part.
The work of the hands
Came from love in her heart.

Now wrap her in love
So she's never alone.
Hold on to her hands –
And escort her home.

We're In There

How deep is the memory?
How deep does it go?
So deep we can't reach it –
More deep than we know.

The store rooms are endless;
The closets are vast;
The pathways are jumbled
Between now and the past.

Which door should we open?
What will we find?
Is there a key to gain access?
And if so, which kind?

The key to a house?
Or a car? Or a skate?
The key to a heart?
Or a mind? Or a gate?

The key is to be there –
Wherever "there" is –
To stay in the moment
And remember this...

Deeper and deeper
Her mind wrestles on.
Deeper still deeper –
We're in there – not gone!

Our mother holds us tightly in her heart and mind.

Remembering Mom

Remembering Mom
  And the laughs that we had,
Choosing to recall
  The happy, not sad....

The baking at Christmas,
  Dinner at 5,
Rooms rearranged –
  The house a beehive.

Hot cocoa in winter
  To take the chill from the storm,
Hand crocheted blankets
  To keep us all warm.

Walks to the park,
  Flowers to smell,
Simple things to enjoy,
  Stories to tell.

Shopping the malls,
  Feeling the fabrics,
Muffins and diet coke,
  Hard to break habits.

Cards on the table –
  No fight or a spat;
"Oops" – there she goes,
  You could bet she'd "buy that"!

Beware the "Mammy Whammy",
*   The cards changed their dots.*
The jokers took cover
*   Or disappeared on the spot.*

We laughed till we cried,
*   Then laughed some more.*
We all were the winners –
*   So who's keeping score?*

Honoring Edna Breeden

Are We There Yet?

I'm going home to see Mom,
  But she is no longer there.
Desperately I start to run
  But to which house, or where?

Anxious to hear her laughter,
  Or just the sound of her voice.
But all I hear is the silence,
  Not so much as the slightest noise.

Tears fall like rain in the forest,
  Leaving their tracks on my face.
Then the reality hits me –
  There is no reason to race.

Mom is wrapped all around me
  As I sit in her flowered robe.
Always a part of who I am –
  With her in my heart, I am home.

THE STIVER FAMILY

Ode to the Young at Heart...

Climbin' the mountain
_____At ninety-three!_
The breath-taking view
_____A sight to see._

A little bit slower –
_____Just to see the sights,_
With a son and a daughter
_____On my left and right._

A river to cross –
_____But the kids say, "No!"_
The rocks are slick,
_____But my heart says, "Go!"_

So we stroll through the woods –
_____There's so much more to see._
So don't stop now –
_____I'm only ninety-three!_

For Loretta

Homespun Vacation

No airplane, or trains,
  No boat, just a car.
Making fun memories
  Is never too far.

A house with a side porch,
  A mountain, a stream,
A lake with a boardwalk –
  Is it real, or a dream?

Skies that are vast
  And the deepest of blue,
Then cap the mountains
  With a white cloud, or two.

No hustle or bustle,
  Just a stroll through the trees –
Watching the colors change
  And the falling of leaves.

Truly on Mountain Time
  Stopping to talk to the locals
Meeting a mountain man
  Who was really quite vocal.

"Nuts about beer"
  Blind Squirrel Brewery – the quest.
Toasting each other
  With some of the best!

October 2013

An apple farm, pumpkins,
  Small shops full of treats,
A hula hoop lesson,
  And eight tired feet.

A week of exploring,
  A sweet goodbye,
Lots of good things remembered,
  Oh, my how time flies.

This homespun vacation
  One of life's mysteries –
Four hearts woven together,
  Into God's tapestry.

Spring in Slocomb

The bareness of winter
  Awakens to spring.
The grey and the brown
  Turning brilliant with green.

The warmth of the sun
  With a chill in the air;
Leaves dance in the breeze
  Without worry or care.

Squirrels play in the brush,
  And birds take to flight.
Wind whispers through the trees
  A song day and night.

Early spring in Slocomb
  Is a sight to see –
Earth in bloom – God's design –
  Simplicity!

Life's hustle and bustle
  Left behind in the rush.
We're enjoying life's best
  From the porch in the hush.

Brothers

Brothers by blood
  and DNA
Really wouldn't have it
  any other way.
A challenge as children
  a struggle, a fight –
One with his left hand,
  the other with his right.
Challenges as young men
  one way then another,
But through it all
  always a brother.
Now old age is the challenge
  yet arm in arm
Climbing on roofs
  keeping each other from harm.
Building together
  as brothers do
A lifetime of memories
  filled with laughter, too.

Dedicated to Bill and Don

Still taking mountains in their 60's!

A Time for All Things

There's a time for all things
    A hello, a goodbye,
A time to embrace,
    And a time to let fly.

A time to be quiet,
    A time to cry out,
A time to whisper,
    And a time to shout!

It's now time to celebrate
    A Mother, a Mom
A lady of grace
    Who made our house a home.

Mom taught us to laugh,
    To love, and to live.
She taught us all how
    To forget and forgive.

Then leaving this life
    Like a night turned to day,
With dignity and grace
    She showed us the way.

With peace in her heart
    She drifted to sleep,
Leaving a legacy behind,
    And wonderful memories to keep.

Yes, there's a time for all things
*   A time to laugh and to cry.*
Soon she'll welcome us home
*   After this brief goodbye.*

Thank you, Mom.
Love, Sue

Honoring Loretta Stiver

**On Monday evening March 23rd Mom passed away
surrounded by her family, she passed with dignity and grace
with a peaceful expression on her beautiful face.**

TO OUR MOTHER, OUR DEAR SWEET MOTHER

Mom protected US, she scolded **US**, she taught **US** right from wrong
She did all the things good mothers do; she wanted **US** to grow up
strong

She taught ME by example how to live my life,
How to be a good mother and a good wife.

She taught me the importance of forgiveness and how to let things go
And to pray to God each day to guide me in the path I should go.

She taught me how to find strength to get through difficult times
To trust there is a bigger picture if I just search between the lines.

She taught me to honor my intuition and to use it in everything I do
If something feels right there's a reason and if it doesn't there's a reason
for that too

She taught me the joy and peace of gardening even on a hot summer's
day
To find the beauty all around us because, God made it that way

She taught me to be happy even though there are sad things from day
to day
To find the humor in a situation even when they are dreary and gray

She taught me to be a lady, to be gracious and content; I know this
was a challenge for her, as many hours we spent.

Mom lived her life in a beautiful and dignified way and continued to teach me lessons even on her very last day.

God provided random weeds and fallen leaves to keep Mom busy near the end but now it's time for someone else to pick up what she began.

I know it is time for you to leave because Ryan and Dad need you too, they need your kind of direction **<u>because Lord knows what they have been up to</u>**.

It's time for you to soar above, I Know I will not be alone.
You will always be with me in everything I do
Now it's time for you to go to the place God has made for you.

I love you Mom, Always and Forever

Your daughter
Gay Louise

You Came

You came to our rescue
     In our time of need.
Thanks for the fuel
     That powered our steed.

Image from Canva Pro

You pushed through the crowds –
     The people seascape,
Filled us with gas
     And made your escape!

So brave and so daring,
     You left without pay.
You even left Kettle Corn
     Behind on that day.

How can we thank you?
     And thank you again?
Here's a treat for your trouble
     In a decorative tin.

Kettle corn for Randy and Lea

The Very Best Gift

There's lots of things to see and do
        During the holiday season,
But family time is the very best –
        And for a very good reason.

It's time to recount blessings
        And the joy throughout the day.
It's time to share our stories
        And things our hearts would say.

It's time to listen closely,
        And time to laugh out loud.
It's time to enjoy each other,
        And leave the busy crowd.

It's time for what's important –
A most precious thing to find.
It's the greatest of all family gifts –
It is the Gift of TIME!

Hokey Pokey

Thank You, Father God, for every moment of every day that we could spend with our families, for all the memories You've given us, and for the minutes and days we still have ahead. Help us to make the most of our togetherness, numbering our days, and sharing all the adventures and stories with our children and grandchildren. Let us leave a legacy of love.

The Kids' Table

The table is set.
>You've called us in.
It's time to dine
>With You again.

The table is low.
>The chairs are small.
The little kids' table
>Is the best of all!

Under the radar,
>Close to the ground,
A vision of God –
>His glory all around.

Free from the worries,
>The cares and the strife,
Free to enjoy the
>Treasures of life.

Then up from the table
>And off to go play,
Remind us we always
>Need three meals a day.

Gathering at Your table
>The tall and the small –
Truly the kids' table
>Is the best of all.

The Prodigal's Plight

It must be exhausting
>*Pushing others away,*
Building up the walls,
>*Holding others at bay.*

It must be exhausting
>*Carrying the weight*
Of all of the anger
>*And all of the hate.*

It must be exhausting
>*To never know why*
Life is all clouded
>*By the tears to be cried.*

It must be exhausting
>*To hold on so tight*
To misunderstandings
>*That started the fight.*

It must be exhausting
>*At the very least*
To walk away from love
>*And sacrifice peace.*

From There They Flew

The tree was full
        Though dark it be.
From there they flew –
        There was no tree!

But there is a tree –
        Though leafless be.
They'll roost again –
        Someday you'll see.

The Family Tree

It ever grows – the Family Tree.
> *Without the growth there'd be no me.*
But I am me as you can see.
> *Oh, how amazing this Family Tree!*

Can't choose the tree from whence I came.
> *Can't take the credit or the blame.*
Wouldn't change a thing, all the same.
> *I love this Tree from whence I came.*

The trunk is wide, the roots are deep.
> *This Family Tree is here for keeps.*
The branches strong, the climb is steep,
> *But it won't fall – the roots are deep.*

Seasons come and seasons go –
> *The leaves, the blooms, the fall, the snow.*
Through the storms – tossed to and fro
> *Still it stays, as seasons go.*

Should saw or ax attack the Tree
> *It would not sever you and me.*
The roots are deeper than you can see.
> *Oh, how amazing this Family Tree.*

A Mother's Day Prayer

Father,

Break the hearts that need breaking;
*   Mend the hearts that are broken.*
Complete the work You've begun;
*   Fulfill the promises You've spoken.*
Take the hearts that are stone
*   And turn them to flesh.*
Return the hearts of the children
*   To the parents' caress.*
Take the words that were twisted
*   And turn them around.*
Dispel the deceit
*   While the Truth can be found.*

Please do what You said –
*   Make everything right.*
The sooner the better
*   Before day turns to night.*
But if it's not sooner
*   Grant me strength as I wait.*
Help me dance in the rain
*   As I look to the gate.*

"Steep your life in God-reality, God-initiative, God-provisions. Don't worry about missing out. You'll find all your everyday human concerns will be met. Give your entire attention to what God is doing right now, and don't get worked up about what may or may not happen tomorrow. God will help you deal with whatever hard things come up when the time comes."
Matthew 6:33-34 (The Message)

Love That Transcends

Scars are a mark that can't be erased.
        Scars are a story, a time, and a place.
They're marks that we bear one way or another.
        Some are obtained just by being a mother.

Surgeons – they'll mend us with staples and stitches,
        Much like a mother repairing torn britches.
But children can wound us so much deeper by far –
        A stab in the heart leaves the worst kind of scar.

No stitches can mend it; the pain's hard to bear –
        But the love's still intact and will always be there.
So when you look at your mother, read the love on her face –
        It's love that transcends all of earth, time, and space!

Mothers are truly remarkable people.
For all mothers:
        May the joys outweigh the sorrows
                and the laughter override the pain.
        May our Heavenly Father grant us strength to stand
                when it seems as though the world is falling around us,
                calm in the midst of the storm, and
                rest in the sleepless nights.

I ask this knowing full well that You, O Lord, have indeed done this for
me over and over and over again. And I am so very grateful!

WORDS

She skillfully wields
> *Her weapons of war –*
Her words as destructive
> *As a two-edged sword.*

Division her purpose,
> *Destruction her goal –*
She harbors an anger
> *Down deep in her soul.*

So out of that anger
> *She wounds as she wills –*
Cutting ties like a mower
> *Over grass that she kills.*

Then gloating in vict'ry
> *Standing in grass that is dead,*
Her heart no less broken
> *By words that she's said.*

To wound out of wounding
> *Is no reason to boast;*
But wound them she must –
> *Ones who love her the most!*

"For I am convinced that neither death, nor life, nor angels, nor principalities, nor things present, nor things to come, nor powers, nor height, nor depth, nor any other created thing will be able to separate us from the love of God that is in Christ Jesus our Lord."
Romans 8:38-39 (NASB)

Anyway

On the good days
        Or the bad –
I love you anyway!

When you're happy
        Or you're sad –
I love you anyway!

With your kind
        Or hurtful words –
I love you anyway!

With your sheathed
        Or lifted sword –
I love you anyway!

Whether outward
        Or in stealth –
I love you anyway!

When you've reached
        The end of self –
I love you anyway!

When the race
        Is finally run,
And all is said
        and done –
I love you anyway!

"I would have despaired unless I had believed that I would see the goodness of the Lord In the land of the living. Wait for the Lord; Be strong and let your heart take courage; Yes, wait for the Lord."
Psalm 27:13-14 (NASB)

"Let angry people endure the backlash of their own anger; if you try to make it better, you'll only make it worse." Proverbs 19:19 (The Message)

"So don't be afraid: I'm with you. I'll round up all your scattered children, pull them in from east and west. I'll send orders north and south: 'Send them back. Return my sons from distant lands, my daughters from faraway places. I want them back, every last one who bears my name, every man, woman, and child whom I created for my glory, yes, personally formed and made each one.'" Isaiah 43:5-7 (The Message)

"I will pour my Spirit into your descendants and my blessing on your children."
Isaiah 44:3 (The Message)

"'All your children will have God for their teacher—
          what a mentor for your children!...
I'll see to it that everything works out for the best.'
          God's Decree."
Isaiah 54:12, 17 (The Message)

Covenant

Remember the stake you drove in the ground –
  A covenant between you and Me?
The stake's still there, and so is My love;
  What I promised will come to be.

I will guard your sons and daughters
  No matter how far they roam.
I will pour My Spirit on them,
  And one day I'll bring them home.

I'll call them in from all four corners –
  From the north, south, east, and west.
Give Me time to work out My plan –
  Not just the good, but My best!

Memory Lane

This year I've been inspired
*   To stroll down Memory Lane.*
Come and take a walk with me
*   While we both still can.*

While our eyes are clear enough
*   And our memories are still sharp –*
Look back with love on those old days,
*   And remember with your heart.*

Remember all the laughter?
*   Listen closely – it's still there!*
The joy is in the "together-times",
*   And the funny stories that we share.*

And share we must those by-gone days –
*   Those treasures before our memory fades.*
How else will they know which cards to play? –
*   When all of us are swept away?*

Our stories are the inspiration
*   For the generations yet to come,*
So they can know that life is good –
*   When all is said and done.*

Play cards. Tell stories. Laugh till you cry!
Most of all remember to pass it on –
Especially if it's The Old Maid!

Ponder Days

Yonder days have become ponder days:
        When did I get my mother's age?
When did my eyesight start to fade?
        When did my body turn the page?
The years they slip by quickly now –
        What I used to could – I can't.
The little kid inside of me
        Says, "let's go!" but knows it shan't.
So in my dreams I jump and run,
        Catch fireflies, and climb trees.
I can do this from the porch swing
        For as many hours as I please.
On the breeze there is a whisper
        That my failing ears can hear,
"I love that child within you
        As I've watched her year to year."
"It's that child that brings Me pleasure."
        Then I recognize the voice –
It's my Father Who created me
        "You are My child. You are My choice."
How can that be? It's only me.
        But my Father says I'm His.
Amazed with awe and wonder
        He gives me days to ponder this.

Now each day becomes a wonder
        Full of thankfulness and praise,
Reflecting on His goodness,
        Enjoying these ponder days!

The Tree

The sky was blue
  And the leaves so green,
The tree I climbed
  Was more than it seemed.
The bark was rough,
  But the limbs were sturdy.
The trunk was stout,
  And the flowers pretty.
So up I climbed
  Into that tree
Just to see
  What I could see.

From that height,
  The house was small.
The clouds were close,
  And I was tall.
The breeze blew
  Stirring all the leaves
As if to say,
  "Come dance with me".
I watched as birds
  Played in the breeze,
Floating in
  And out of trees.
T'was there I dreamt
  that I could fly –
Just like the birds
  Up in the sky.

The tree became
        A dreaming place,
A world of wonder –
        My escape...

The years have passed
        The tree is gone,
But I'm still here
        And life goes on.

Too old to climb,
        But not to ponder.
My mind takes flight
        And starts to wonder.

When I Am Old

When I am old
        And can't remember your name,
Please know that
        I love you just the same.

When words get jumbled
        And thoughts are unclear,
Please understand
        The "me" is still here.

The girl that would run
        And look to the sky,
Dance in the rain –
        She still longs to fly.

And fly she will –
        Her mind finally free.
Look into her heart,
        And know it's still "me".

The rainbow – God's promise –
        His love ever true.
A heart full of hope
        I'm passing to you.

So when I am old
        And can't remember your name,
Please know that
        I love you just the same.

A Place Beyond

I know there is a place beyond
Every doubt and fear.
A place where joy can override
Every hurt and tear.

A place where hearts can understand
What words alone can't say.
A place so deep, and love so strong
It can't be explained away.

A place so near and yet so far ...
A pathway with no stairs.
A place beyond our wildest dreams ...
Perhaps I'll meet you there.

What's the Rush?

Linger here a little longer.
*   Rest in Me. I'll make you stronger.*
Watch the breeze blow through the trees.
*   Watch Me dance among the leaves.*
Then close your eyes and take My hand,
*   And we will dance as lovers can –*
Heart-to-Heart and Face-to-Face
*   Captured in the sweet embrace.*
Hear Me whisper in your ear,
*   "You're the treasure I hold most dear."*

I want to say, "How can that be?
*   Who am I? It's only me."*
But the words could not come out,
*   You held me close, erased all doubt.*
And so, I'll rest in Your embrace.
*   For me there is no better place.*

Thank you, God, for asking the question,
having this conversation, and the dance.
You are my heart's desire.
12 November 2023

New Perspective

In times of great loss,
> *Grief comes in like waves crashing on the seashore.*

Desperately I asked God,
> *"When will the waves end?"*

He so tenderly answered,
> *"If there were no waves,*
> *there'd be no sound on the beach."*

To which I replied,
> *"Lord, I have always loved that sound."*

And He smiled.

The "Other" Place

You've brought us to an "Other" Place,
*   Beyond all we can see and feel –*
A place where time does not exist,
*   Yet it's a place that is so real.*

My head says, "This cannot be so
*   In a world that's so dark and drear."*
My heart says, "Where else would we go?
*   Why would we want to leave here?"*

So often we'd visit that "Other" Place
*   And share what He showed us there.*
We'd sit and talk for hours
*   About His tender loving care.*

Our visits got more intimate
*   As we met God day to day.*
We longed to be in His presence.
*   Oh, how we'd wish we could stay.*

So, stay you did in that "Other" Place.
*   Your heart's desire was to see His face.*
You ran the course, and finished the race.
*   One day I'll join you, by His grace.*

Dedicated to my husband, Don, who met his Creator face to face
on February 13th 2024.

Roll with the Tide

Roll with the tide.
    Ride on the waves.
Row with your strength
    All of your days.

Coast in the calm,
    But always aware.
Learn to read clouds
    When the weather is fair.

Know there'll be storms.
    Prepare to be tossed.
Row like a team,
    Or all will be lost.

Ocean or river –
    Enjoy the ride!
Laugh through the journey
    As you roll with the tide.

Thank You

Thank you for joining me in the ebb and flow of life and family.
Ride the waves, stroll on the beaches, find the treasures in the sand.
Be refreshed.

Thanks be to God
For the gift of rhyme,
And how He has used it
Time after time
to gather my thoughts,
to express my heart,
to settle my fears,
giving me a fresh start.

This book in your hands
Is His gift to you
To be read and then shared
With others, too.

About the Author

Susan Stiver is a multifaceted diamond in the rough. From her first wall art with red lipstick, to poetry, sketching, a 40-year career in Neonatal Nursing, motherhood, photography, and mixed media art, this lump of coal now has a superabundance of life treasures to expound upon in literary form. Her passion is to communicate the heart of God through her writing and art, expressing God's love and desire for each individual to know and be known by Him.

In this world, where at times, it seems there is no rhyme or reason, Susan has found that she has been given rhyme for a reason. For her it has been a creative expression to convey thoughts, questions, and muses that inspire and encourage others. Her poetry is a dance with words, scribing heart-whispers on paper with ink.

The world is so full of God-wonders. Step into this writer's world, and find the treasures in the sand.

Contact the Author: Susanstiver212@gmail.com

Also by Susan Stiver

He Loves You to Pieces

A Heart Stirred for Fellowship
Co-authored with her husband
Don Stiver

A Walk in the Garden
Go Beyond Me Series
Book One

www.ingramcontent.com/pod-product-compliance
Lightning Source LLC
Chambersburg PA
CBHW051155120626
46547CB00012B/1073